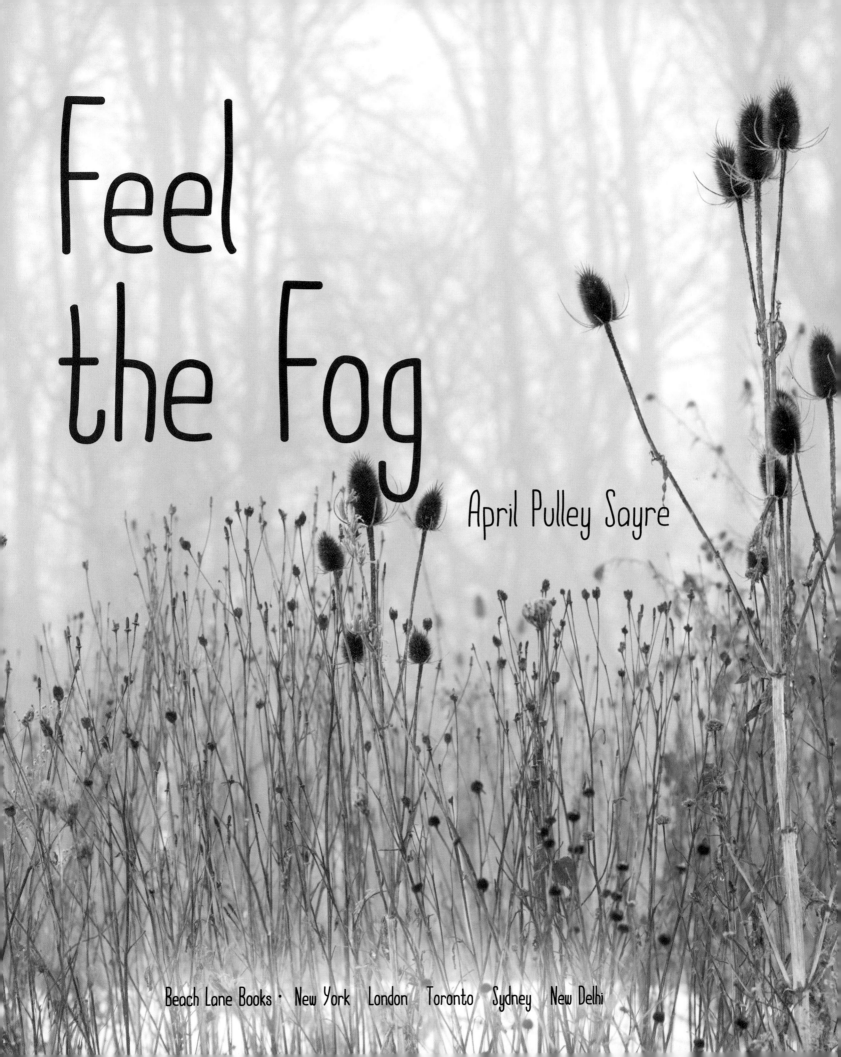

Feel the Fog

April Pulley Sayre

Beach Lane Books · New York London Toronto Sydney New Delhi

Fog rolls in,
damp and pale.

A cloud, ground level,
hugs stone

and snail.

It swallows the distant.

Details dim.

Colors gray.

Lights glow. Barely show.

Squint to find the way.

Feel the fog.

Dewy. Cold stewy.

Dank and drippy.

Plip,

plop,

plippy.

Wherever air,
moist and warm,
begins to cool,

fog may form.

Sun-warmed air,
after sunset, cools.

Lowland fog
layers and pools.

Warm, wet wind
meets cold lakes,

cold seas.

Fog plays peekaboo
with ridges

and trees.

Thicker than mist,

fog can drift,
fog can flow.

Fog forms above
fields of snow.

Fog shifts focus

to near, right here.

Water in the air

cools,

condenses.

Forms flap.

Silhouettes sing

from wires and fences.

Wisps waft, lift aloft.

A peek of blue.
Air warms and dries.

Will sun burn through?

Not here.
Not today.

Hooray!

Feel the fog.

Fog: The Clouds That Come to Visit

Fog-filled air changes how the landscape looks. It scatters colors. It dims details. Yet it can also highlight shapes. A foggy daytime stroll feels like a walk through a poem or an ink wash painting.

Fog is actually a cloud at ground level. Like clouds up in the sky, fog is mostly air mixed with tiny water droplets or ice crystals. Dust and other particles and gases can float in fog, too.

Why Objects in Fog Look Pale

When you see an object, your eyes sense light that bounces off that object. Light that bounces off a distant object must travel a long way to reach your eyes. Along the way, air scatters some of that light, so distant objects may appear pale. All that happens in clear air. In foggy air, water droplets and ice crystals scatter even more light, so objects may appear even paler. Or you may not see them at all.

Disappearing in the Distance

Fog limits visibility—how far an average person can see—to less than a kilometer (.62 miles). When an object disappears into the fog, it is still there, of course. But our eyes can no longer see the difference between its shape and the background.

The Invisible Water around You

Even on a clear day, water vapor floats in the air. Water vapor is the invisible gaseous form of water.

When water vapor comes into contact with something cool, it may condense, forming droplets. It is turning from a gas into a liquid. Water droplets bead on the outsides of water glasses, water pipes, and air conditioners. This water isn't from inside an object. It's water vapor from the air that has condensed on the cooled outside surface.

When Moist, Warm Air Meets Cool

Condensation also happens when moist, warm air from your lungs meets cold air. The water vapor in your breath condenses, forming droplets in the air—a tiny cloud.

Warm meets cold on a larger scale in winter. Moist, water-vapor-filled air meets cold seawater, cold land, or a cold-air weather front. Droplets form on dust particles in the air. The air temperature at which these droplets form is called the *dew point*. When air cools to the dew point, the droplets become dew, mist, fog, rain, or snow.

Fog after Rain and Steam Fog

Although fog mostly happens in cool conditions, it can also form on a warm day during and after rainfall. The rain falling through the air cools the air, changing its dew point, so fog forms.

Fog can also form when river water, lake water, or seawater evaporates. It looks like steam rising from the water. But it's not hot like steam is.

How Does Fog Clear?

Fog clears when the air temperature or air pressure changes. Sun can heat the air and dry it. Or wind can push fog out of the way or help mix it with warmer or drier air. Yet fog may return the next day. Although fog can form at any time, it often forms in the cool of the night and is visible the next morning.

Why Does Fog Feel Cold?

Fog often forms in cool conditions, so it's no wonder that it can feel a bit chilly. But there's another reason for that feeling. Water absorbs more heat from your skin than air does. (A swimming pool that's 70 degrees Fahrenheit may chill you, yet 70-degree air feels just fine.) Foggy air, which is full of water droplets, makes your skin feel cooler than dry air at the same temperature.

The Sound of Fog

If you live on the seacoast, you may hear a foghorn. Foghorns groan, blasting sounds to warn sailors. Before modern sailing instruments, many ships ran aground during foggy nights and days. That's because the sailors could not see that land was nearby and the water was shallow.

Even if you do not live near a foghorn, a foggy day can change what you hear. Water droplets in the air scatter not just light waves, but also sound waves. A sound may seem muffled. And it can be harder to tell where it originates.

The Wild Wonders of Fog

In Africa's Namib desert, beetles harvest fog. Head down, beetles tilt their backs up to catch fog that rolls in off the ocean. The fog beads up on each beetle's back and slides down grooves toward its mouth.

In South America's Atacama Desert, people have built tall nets that face the sea. When fog rolls inland, it beads up on the nets and flows down into storage tanks. This water can be used for drinking and watering crops.

What other inventions will fog inspire? What will fog teach us about light, smell, or sound? A foggy day is a great time to notice and explore. Fog limits what you can see, but it can expand what you imagine.

For all who venture out in the elements—
especially ski patrollers Cathy, Eli, Virginia, and Cat

Acknowledgments

Thank you to my brother-in-law Rodney Willett and nephew Turner Willett
for the use of two Greenland iceberg-and-fog photos. Gratitude to Sam
Lashley, senior meteorologist for the National Weather Service, for reviewing
the text. For foggy hospitality, thank you to the Willett family, Jamie Hogan,
Barb Crighton, and John Huemmer, and thanks to Karyn Lewis Bonfiglio,
who called me on fog-warning days. For foggy inspiration, thank you to the
staff at St. Patrick's County Park in Indiana; the Canopy Tower in Panama's
rain forest; the volunteers at the Venice Area Audubon Rookery in Venice,
Florida; the residents of Portland, Maine; the road maintenance crews of
the Pennsylvania Turnpike and Route 81; and the Wintergreen Resort in
Virginia. Thank you to Andrea Welch, Allyn Johnston, Rebecca Syracuse,
Lauren Rille, Elizabeth Blake-Linn, Bridget Madsen, Sarah Jane Abbott,
Anne Zafian, Jon Anderson, and the entire Beach Lane/S&S team.

BEACH LANE BOOKS
An imprint of Simon & Schuster Children's Publishing Division
1230 Avenue of the Americas, New York, New York 10020
Copyright © 2020 by April Pulley Sayre
All rights reserved, including the right of reproduction in whole or in part in any form.
BEACH LANE BOOKS is a trademark of Simon & Schuster, Inc.
For information about special discounts for bulk purchases, please contact Simon & Schuster Special Sales
at 1-866-506-1949 or business@simonandschuster.com.
The Simon & Schuster Speakers Bureau can bring authors to your live event. For more information or to book an event,
contact the Simon & Schuster Speakers Bureau at 1-866-248-3049 or visit our website at www.simonspeakers.com.
Book design by Rebecca Syracuse
The text for this book was set in QuickRest.
Manufactured in China
0620 SCP
First Edition
10 9 8 7 6 5 4 3 2 1
Library of Congress Cataloging-in-Publication Data
Names: Sayre, April Pulley, author.
Title: Feel the fog / April Pulley Sayre.
Description: New York : Beach Lane Books, an imprint of Simon & Schuster Children's Publishing Division, [2020] |
Audience: Ages 3–8. | Audience: Grades 2–3. | Summary: "A photographic picture book that explores how fog is formed,
how it clears away, why it feels cold, and more"—Provided by publisher.
Identifiers: LCCN 2019055465 (print) | ISBN 9781534437609 (hardcover) | ISBN 9781534437616 (eBook)
Subjects: LCSH: Fog—Juvenile literature. | Meteorology—Juvenile literature. | LCGFT: Picture books.
Classification: LCC QC929.F7 S29 2020 (print) | DDC 551.57/5—dc23
LC record available at https://lccn.loc.gov/2019055465